At Risk of Foreclosure?

I0828395

10 WAYS TO SAVE YOUR HOME FROM FORECLOSURE

KNOW THE WAYS TO BE SAVED

- ✓ PERSONAL LOANS
- ✓ AGENT LISTING
- ✓ LOAN MODIFICATION
- ✓ RENTAL
- ✓ CASH OFFER
- ✓ CREATIVE FINANCING
- ✓ RENOVATE & LIST
- ✓ DEED IN LIEU
- ✓ FORBEARANCE
- ✓ BANKRUPTCY

Published by Simms Books Publishing Corporation

Jonesboro, GA

Copyright ©THE B ALEXIS GROUP, LLC, 2021

All rights reserved. No part of this book may be reproduced, scanned, or distributed in any print or electronic form without permission. Please do not participate in or encourage piracy of copyrighted materials in violation of the author's rights. Purchase only authorized editions.

Library of Congress Cataloging in Publication Data

201*******

10 WAYS TO SAVE YOUR HOME FROM FORECLOSURE

ISBN: 978-1-949433-12-8

Printed in the United States of America

Book Arrangement by THE B ALEXIS GROUP, LLC

SIMMS BOOKS PUBLISHING CORPORATION

Editor: Cortnie Hines

Table of Contents

1. What is Foreclosure? 1
2. The consequences of foreclosure 3
3. The process of foreclosure 4
4. The Starting Steps 5
5. 10 Ways to Save your Home from Foreclosure 7

- Personal Loans 7
- Agent Listing (Short Sale) 8
- Loan Modification 10
- Rental 12
- Cash Offer 13
- Subject To / Creative Financing 13
- Renovate & List 14
- Deed in Lieu of Foreclosure 15
- Forbearance 17
- Bankruptcy 18

6. Conclusion 19

1. What is Foreclosure?

When your home is valued lower than the outstanding balance you owe, leaving your home voluntarily might seem to be the most reasonable solution. However, the financial consequences that come with doing so, may not be in your best interest. Even after your home is listed for foreclosure, some states will continue to require homeowners to make partial payments.

Your credit rating will also be negatively affected if you choose to foreclose your home, making renting or purchasing a home more difficult in the future. Researching options, other than foreclosure, would be best, to avoid having to experience a foreclosure.

Favorable, and unassuming, foreclosure is the last process that your mortgage company wants to endure, as the execution of a foreclosure proves to be a costly and time-consuming ordeal. It is in the best interest of your mortgage company and you, the homeowner, to receive payment on your balance. Unfortunately, many homeowners default on such alternatives, and inevitably foreclose becomes the only option.

As a homeowner, you want to keep and protect your home, and it is imperative that you know your options when making payments gets tough. Foreclosure can be avoided if you know and utilize what is in place to help you. Some homeowners choose to avoid their situation, and time expires to use any other option, and foreclosure is then unavoidable. The bottom line is that foreclosure can cause perpetual and negative consequences to the former homeowner.

By definition, a foreclosure is a legal process by which your mortgage company takes possession of your home, similar to a repossession. When the homeowner defaults on their mortgage, by not making the scheduled payments, the mortgage company issues a foreclosure to repossess the property.

Did you already receive a notice of foreclosure? It is still not too late to explore your options, which are found in this E-book.

You need to take action now!

2. The consequences of foreclosure

The main consequences of foreclosure:

Eviction from the home—You will ultimately have to leave your home and any accumulated equity as well. In times of uncertainty, not knowing how you and your family will progress, eviction can be quite stressful.

- **Damage to credit**—Adverse credit decisions and the inability to be approved for new crediting or future financing, as well as not being offered some employment opportunities, foreclosure can cause severe damage to your credit.

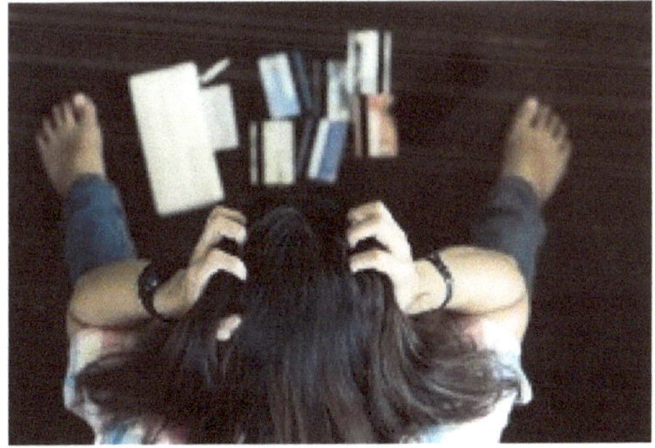

3. The process of foreclosure

Foreclosure is presented in two categories:

- **Judicial** – A formal legal proceeding, supervised and led by the court (also known as a civil lawsuit)
- **Non-judicial** – Cases that are not court-supervised.

Regardless of the category under which the foreclosure falls, the homeowner will in same, receive a notice of the impending foreclosure. You, the homeowner, should also know that the notice of your foreclosure is not only published in the local newspaper, but it is then sold at a public auction, and would be coordinated by the court if it is a judicial foreclosure. Depending on your state's laws, the process and length of time the foreclosure may take will vary. Commonly, **two months (60 days)** after the homeowner fails to make payment, the mortgage company can initiate the foreclosure process. Once a homeowner is aware of possible delinquency, it is imperative that they take Immediate Action and communicate with the mortgage company to discuss options to resolve the matter in the timeliest fashion. Time is of the essence, and as the figure below illustrates, once the home is

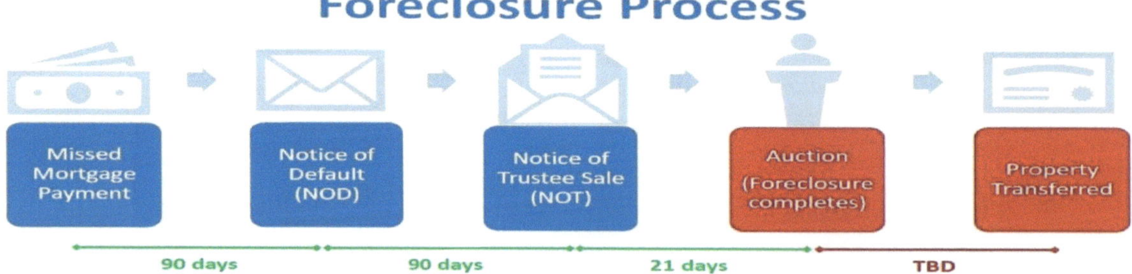

placed up for auction, foreclosure is imminent, unavoidable. That's why it is strongly recommended for the homeowner to contact their mortgage company and research the options that will best aid them in this trying time, and help them avoid going through the process of losing their home.

4. The Starting Steps

As a homeowner, the following steps will guide you through the process of avoiding foreclosure:

1. Gather all financial data

Before contacting your mortgage company, being prepared with your basic financial documents and information, will lend to a less stressful interaction. Here are some of the documents you should have:

- Mortgage statements
- Second mortgage information (if applicable)
- Monthly debt payments (such as a car or student loans, personal loan, credit card payments, etc.)
- Monthly and annual income details (pay stubs and income tax returns)

2. Understand your current status

By outlining your existing hardships and being in a position to confidently present your current situation in as much detail as possible. When contacting your mortgage company, be aware that you will have to discuss and explain why you are unable to make your payments, as promised, along with disclosing any foreseeable financial hardships you may face. Your mortgage company now has information that can help them help you. They would review what you had discussed and later present you with options to try and help you avoid foreclosure, leaving that to be the final option. With the understanding of your situation, you and your mortgage company may be able to find the appropriate compromise to satisfy both parties.

5. 10 Ways to Save your Home from Foreclosure

Once you become more familiar with the definition, process, and terms of foreclosure, you will be able to determine what stage you are currently in, in the foreclosure process. Having a better understanding will in fact increase your odds of making the most informed decisions, and support your efforts in avoiding foreclosure. Now equipped with the foundation, you are ready to explore the top 10 proven ways to avoid the foreclosure and save your home, that are as follows:

- **Personal Loans**

The mortgage company might provide the homeowner with the opportunity to enter into a short refinance loan, in which the lender forgives part of the balance owed and recalculates an entirely new loan, with terms more feasible for your current financial situation. However, if the mortgage company deems the homeowner to be too high-risk, thus leaving this option off of the table, there is still hope.

The next option would involve applying for a refinance loan with a private lender, other than your current mortgage company. However, this option will come with its own terms of payment, interest, and fees, all of which can be very costly. However, the goal is to buy time and you will ultimately be able to keep your house while paying off the new loan. At this time, it may be wise to call upon friends and family for assistance, any little financial relief they can provide the better for you.

Refinancing your mortgage using a personal loan is a great option, especially if you still own equity in your home and your credit has not yet been negatively affected by the current foreclosure process. Some wonderful programs, to help unemployed or homeowners who have high debt to obtain loan modification and refinancing, are offered by Department of Housing and Urban Development (HUD) .

- **Agent Listing (Short Sale)**

In some cases, with the help of a real-estate agent the homeowner may have the opportunity to sell their home for a lower value. Providing the homeowner with the opportunity to pay the lender with the proceeds from the sale, and having the remaining debt resolved.

The initiation of a short sale is done by the property owner, usually occurring after realizing that making a mortgage payment would be impossible. Space different from state-to-state, the following steps are generally involved when proceeding with a short sale:

- **Short sale package** – The homeowner submits a financial package to the lender. This entails copies of all related financial records and a letter explaining the homeowner's hardship.
- **Listing** – Upon approval of the short sale request by the lender, the homeowner works with the reliable and expert foreclosure real estate agent to get the home listed. They will also make a sales contract to be approved by the lender.
- **Short sale offer** – If an interested buyer bids a good offer, the listing agent sends these documents to the lender: the buyer's preapproval letter; an implemented purchase agreement, and a copy of the earnest money check.
- **Bank processing** – The financial institution evaluates the offer and will either approve or deny the short sale.

*Unlike foreclosure, short sales do not negatively impact your credit rating and therefore are worth the effort and intensity of the lengthy process.

- **Loan Modification**

Requesting a permanent or temporary change in your mortgage agreement, also known as a loan modification, is also an option that your mortgage company can offer. Most mortgage companies would rather provide you a loan modification than proceed with the foreclosure of your home. This is, in part, due to the process of loan modifications being a rather less expensive and extensive process when compared with foreclosure.

The process of loan modification involves your mortgage lender either increasing the amortization schedule, rolling a delinquent amount into an existing loan, or decreasing the interest rate, in order to help you bring the loan current.

Mortgage modification options:

- **Principal reduction** – Define by its name, this is the process of having your principal reduced and future payments would be based on that reduction.
- **Lower interest rate** – Providing you with the result of abridged monthly payments, the lender could lower your interest rates.
- **Extended-term** – Giving you more time to pay the loan, the lender would extend the term of your loan.

- **Fixed-rate loan** – If you are eligible, you may be able to have your adjustable-rate loan change to a fixed rate loan, and that's giving you a lower interest rate at the same time. interest rate.
- **Postponed payments** – in cases of unexpected unemployment or medical emergencies, a lender may propose you to temporarily pause your mortgage payment until your financial situation improves.

- ## Rental

Before approaching the final stages of foreclosure, the options of the homeowner to rent their home out to roommate or hosting their home on room sharing websites like Airbnb, or simply relocating and renting the home out entirely, would provide income for the homeowner to make mortgage payments in an economical way and thus avoid foreclosure. However, keep in mind that this option requires the homeowner to become a temporary landlord.

- **Cash Offer**

Selling your house for cash is similar to a short sell because it protects your credit. However, with this option you will be able to more flexibly set your own time frame and have more say over the price for the sale of your home.

- **Subject To / Creative Financing**

When practicing uncommon and non-traditional means of buying land or property in real estate, it is referred to as creative financing. with the goal of using or investing as little money as possible, creative financing is possible and is commonly known as acquiring OPM space (Other People's Money). Using the OPM method is beneficial to those knowledgeable investors as they really have to use little of their own money when purchasing multiple properties.

Another creative finance technique is called a subject-to transaction. This takes place when a seller is involved in a transaction of assuming another loan without its existing financial institution being aware of the transaction. Similarly, to assuming a loan but differing with the fact that there's no need for transaction costs and capital to obtain the new loan. The buyer also has the ability to quickly purchase without going through the long and arduous loan origination process. A great benefit of using this process includes the fact that the credit of the seller will not be ruined but saved because payments would be made on time.

- **Renovate & List**

Keeping your home in good condition and being aggressive when selling improves and speeds up the selling process, even in a tough housing market. More quickly you sell your house the better chance you have of reducing the loss you can suffer in the event of a foreclosure. Budgeting for renovations and repairs and advance to any type of hardship is the key to this option.

• Deed in Lieu of Foreclosure

By now you know that foreclosure, in its Essence, means repossession.

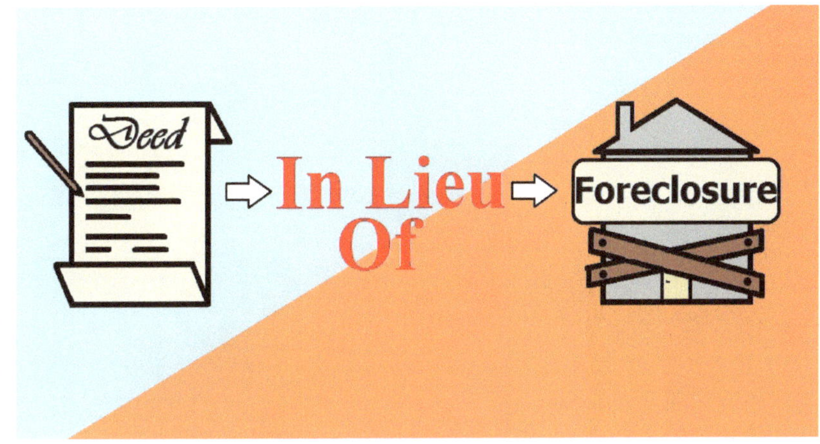

Therefore, you do not have to let the mortgage company seize your property, you can give it back. This is called a deed-in-lieu of foreclosure. If the previous options failed to suffice as viable, your mortgage lender will take your deed and exchange 4 your release from the debt that you owe, even if it cost them more to do so.

Yes, technically a deed-in-lieu is still a type of foreclosure however the benefit is the home owner's ability to avoid the public embarrassment that usually comes with the process of formal foreclosure proceedings.

Also, your credit will still be hurt by participating in a deed-in-lieu of foreclosure but you will be able to move to your next steps more immediately than you would if you went through the lengthy legal process of the actual foreclosure rather it is deemed a judicial or non-judicial foreclosure. Furthermore, who is a mortgage company but foreclosure you would have to wait a minimum of five years before you could think about purchasing another house, the benefit of using the deed in lieu of foreclosure auction can reduce that time frame by 3 years or more.

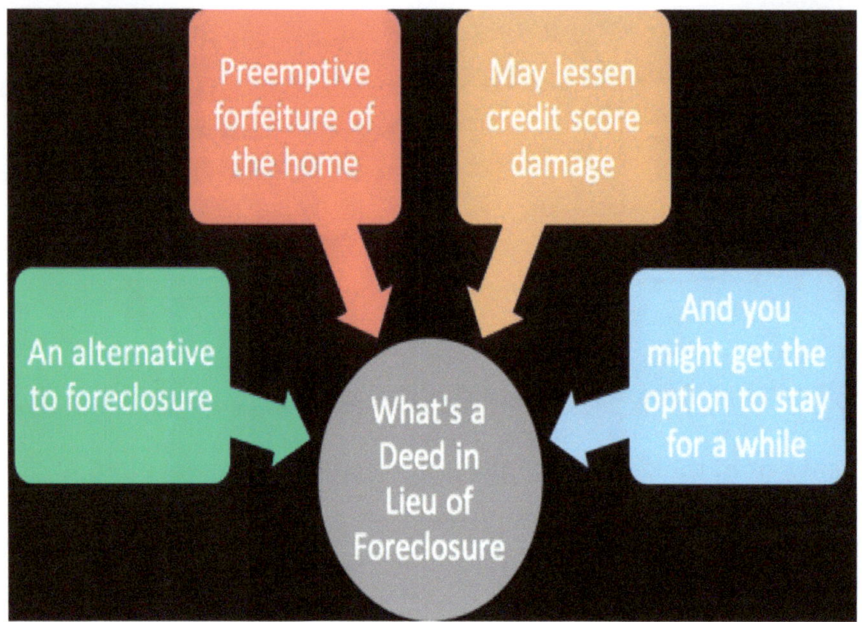

- **Forbearance**

And Times of extenuating circumstances for example this time of COVID-19, many homeowners have not been able to pay their bills more specifically their mortgages and rent due to the layoffs caused by the pandemic. However, some mortgage lenders, most rather, are offering a forbearance option. Forbearance is when the mortgage lender can suspend the homeowner's mortgage payments for a temporary amount of time until the financial security is restored. However, this does not release the homeowner from any responsibilities as they would have to still pay the money that was temporarily suspended. Most forbearance agreement will require the homeowner to make a promise to repay the suspended payment and, in some cases, pay more to catch up on the interest.

The same way you would seek a loan modification from your mortgage company would be the same process a homeowner with use to request a forbearance. You would simply contact your lender and ask them to help you set up the forbearance plan. Please keep in mind that forbearance is only temporary; it will not save you from what you may no longer be able to afford.

- **Bankruptcy**

1 costly but sure-fire way to stop foreclosure in its tracks is to file for bankruptcy. Bankruptcy is a petition in which you file with the federal courts that you are no longer able to pay your debts and would like them to serve a cease-and-desist to all credit collections. However, this is not a resolution to the loss of your home. This is simply a platform where you, the debtor, and the lender can receive mediation regarding the foreclosure. This provides time for you the homeowner to find means to pay your debt. Lawfully it is the responsibility of you and your mortgage company to come to a reasonable resolution and formulate a repayment plan so that you can resolve your issues. If at all possible, it is highly suggested that you hire a bankruptcy attorney so that they can assist you with making the best decisions and moving forward with your Current financial situation. Again, bankruptcy only stops the process of foreclosure until you and the lender can come to an agreement. If no agreement is possible, the

ultimate result would still be the loss of your home. Bankruptcy should be the absolute final decision before succumbing to a foreclosure. it will impact your credit negatively and calls you some of the same issues as the impending foreclosure. With that said, use this option when you feel that you will eventually be able to repay your debts and avoid foreclosure.

6. Conclusion

Breathe. Don't panic. You now have the tools and are aware of your options. Dealing with foreclosure or the risk thereof can be a very stressful process. But, taking immediate action and developing your best options to make the best decisions can help you to forecast and prevent any future possibilities of foreclosure. Remember to be proactive by staying abreast of all of the options that are provided to you in order to help you save your home. If you do have to experience a foreclosure, when you are capable of buying another home use the knowledge from this experience and do not enter into any mortgage that you could not potentially afford. It is wise to make sure you have more money than you need just in case the unexpected happens. The monthly payment of your home should not exceed more than 28% of your income. This wonderful rule to live by and most people that do rarely have to face impending foreclosures. Do not be ashamed. Learn from your mistakes and do better in the future. Sometimes, even when you've done all you can the worst can happen oh, but you must do all you can and with this eBook you have the plan and the tools it is up to you to implement them.

The B Alexis Group LLC has helped families avoid foreclosure.

Do you owe more money than your home is worth? The B Alexis Group LLC understands that homeownership may cause financial challenges and create burdens. If your lender won't stop calling and you feel overwhelmed, let us help. If you are facing hardship and behind on your mortgage payments, call on us. We are here to help. Have you received a foreclosure notice from your lender, or are you currently in the pre foreclosure process? Give us a call. We've helped many homeowners in delinquency situations to be relieved of their remaining mortgage debt, and some homeowners even walk away with relocation assistance.

We understand that you may feel like you are out of options and alone, but you are not. Let our trusted team of foreclosure solution specialists help guide you through the process and begin taking the steps to financial freedom. Don't wait – the traditional real estate process can take months, but we can offer you quick and effective solutions today.

Start the conversation now to get the best scenario advice to deal with your foreclosure risk. Schedule a personal call to discuss further at 1**-877-278-2023**.

www.ingramcontent.com/pod-product-compliance
Lightning Source LLC
LaVergne TN
LVHW070208110826
845147LV00002B/536

* 9 7 8 1 9 4 9 4 3 3 1 2 8 *